PACHYCEPHALOSAURUS

A Buddy Book
by
Michael P. Goecke

ABDO
Publishing Company

VISIT US AT

www.abdopublishing.com

Published by ABDO Publishing Company, 4940 Viking Drive, Edina, Minnesota 55435.

Edited by: Sarah Tieck
Graphic Design: Denise Esner
Cover Art: Luis Rey, title page
Interior Photos/Illustrations: Page 5: Natural History Museum; pages 7, 15, 21 & 23: photos.com; pages 8 & 9: ©Julius T. Csotonyi, image modified by publisher; page 11: ©Julius T. Csotonyi; page 13: Luis Rey; page 17: Joe Tucciarone; page 18: Getty Images News; page 22: John Sibbick; page 25: Hulton Archive/Getty Images; page 26: Carnegie Museum of Natural History.

Library of Congress Cataloging-in-Publication Data

Goecke, Michael P., 1968-
  Pachycephalosaurus / Michael P. Goecke.
    p. cm. (Dinosaurs)
  Includes index.
  ISBN-13: 978-1-59928-699-0
  ISBN-10: 1-59928-699-8
  1. Pachycephalosaurus—Juvenile literature. I. Title.

QE862.O65G636 2007
567.914—dc22
                                                          2006032071

TABLE OF CONTENTS

WHAT WAS IT?

Millions of years ago, the world was a very different place. Dinosaurs roamed the earth. One very strange dinosaur was called the Pachycephalosaurus. This dinosaur lived 65 million years ago, during the Late **Cretaceous period**.

**Pachycephalosaurus
PAK-uh-SEHF-uh-luh-SAWR-uhs**

The Pachycephalosaurus wasn't as big as some dinosaurs. But, it was still large! It measured between 13 and 26 feet (four and eight m) long. And, the Pachycephalosaurus may have weighed between 950 and 2,000 pounds (430 and 910 kg).

The Pachycephalosaurus probably weighed as much as a modern-day polar bear!

Scientists use **fossils** to gather information about dinosaurs.

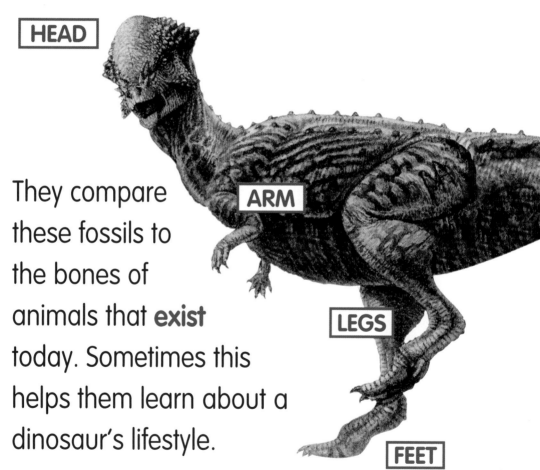

HEAD

ARM

LEGS

FEET

They compare these fossils to the bones of animals that **exist** today. Sometimes this helps them learn about a dinosaur's lifestyle.

Very few Pachycephalosaurus **fossils** have been found. Based on the few fossils scientists have, they claim the Pachycephalosaurus walked on its two hind legs. These legs were thick and strong. However, the Pachycephalosaurus probably wasn't a very fast runner.

TAIL

WHY WAS IT SPECIAL?

The Pachycephalosaurus was an **unusual** dinosaur. The top of its **skull** resembled a helmet. It was up to ten inches (25 cm) thick and surrounded by horns. It almost looked like a crown.

The Pachycephalosaurus might have used its thick skull to push other dinosaurs around.

What did the Pachycephalosaurus use its thick **skull** for? At first, scientists thought it rammed heads with other Pachycephalosaurus dinosaurs.

Scientists studied the Pachycephalosaurus **fossils** more. They decided that its neck could not have handled such force. Both dinosaurs would have been badly injured.

No one knows for sure why the Pachycephalosaurus had such a thick **skull**. Some scientists think it was for protection against enemies. Others believe it was used to attract a mate.

The Pachycephalosaurus's thick skull and short horns might have been a sign of strength to other Pachycephalosaurus dinosaurs.

13

LAND OF THE PACHYCEPHALOSAURUS

The Pachycephalosaurus lived mostly in western North America. North America was very different in the Late **Cretaceous period**. A shallow sea divided the **continent**. Because of this, some land was under water.

During the Late **Cretaceous period**, North America was probably warm all year. Today, the **continent** has seasons and is not always warm.

Today, North America experiences all four seasons. It is no longer warm year-round.

The Pachycephalosaurus lived among many **herbivorous** dinosaurs. One of these was the Triceratops.

The Triceratops was a ceratopsian dinosaur. Often, these dinosaurs had horns. The Triceratops had one horn above each eye. An additional shorter horn sat on its nose.

Some scientists think that Pachycephalosaurus might have been a ceratopsian, like the Triceratops.

Some scientists claim the Pachycephalosaurus is related to the Triceratops. This is because the two dinosaurs share important features.

Triceratops fossils can be seen at the American Museum of Natural History in New York City.

The Triceratops had thick bone on its head, like the Pachycephalosaurus. This hard plate covered the back of the **skull** and protected the neck. Scientists call this plate a frill.

WHAT DID IT EAT?

Scientific **theories** suggest that the Pachycephalosaurus was an **herbivore**. It may have used its front teeth to tear apart tough plants. Some of these were flowering plants called angiosperms.

The Pachycephalosaurus's teeth suggest it may have also eaten insects and seeds. It probably also enjoyed the fruit of angiosperms, such as figs.

Apple trees are an example of a modern-day angiosperm.

WHO WERE ITS ENEMIES?

An adult T. rex could be as much as 46 feet (14 m) long!

The Tyrannosaurus rex was a big dinosaur. It was a **carnivore**. It had sharp teeth and claws. The T. rex was a fast and powerful hunter. It probably hunted the Pachycephalosaurus.

Many scientists believe that the Pachycephalosaurus was a herd animal. Herd animals travel in large groups. They share the jobs of looking out for **predators** and finding food.

Some modern-day herd animals include wildebeests and antelope. These animals live in Africa.

Wildebeest herds roam the plains in search of food.

DISCOVERY

   In 1938, a rancher named William Winkley discovered the first Pachycephalosaurus **fossil**. Winkley found the fossilized Pachycephalosaurus **skull** on his family's ranch near Ekalaka, Montana.

   Scientists Barnum Brown and Erich M. Schlaikjer studied the fossil. They named the dinosaur Pachycephalosaurus in 1943.

Barnum Brown helped unearth many dinosaur fossils.

25

The discovery of Sandy helped scientists learn even more about the Pachycephalosaurus.

In 1994, **fossil** collector Mike Triebold found the first **partial** Pachycephalosaurus fossil skeleton. Before this discovery, few other Pachycephalosaurus fossils had been found. And, most of these were just fossilized **skull** pieces.

The skeleton Triebold discovered was only nine feet (three m) long. He nicknamed it Sandy. Sandy is the most complete Pachycephalosaurus skeleton that has been found.

Carnegie Museum of Natural History
4400 Forbes Avenue
Pittsburgh, PA 15213
http://www.carnegiemnh.org

PACHYCEPHALOSAURUS

NAME MEANS	Thick-headed lizard
DIET	Plants
WEIGHT	950 to 2,000 pounds (430-910 kg)
LENGTH	13 to 26 feet (4-8 m)
TIME	Late Cretaceous period
SPECIAL FEATURE	Very thick skull on top of its head
FOSSILS FOUND	Montana and Canada

The Pachycephalosaurus
lived 65 million years ago.

The first humans appeared
1.6 million years ago.

Triassic Period	Jurassic Period	Cretaceous Period	Tertiary Period
245 Million years ago	208 Million years ago	144 Million years ago	65 Million years ago
Mesozoic Era			Cenozoic Era

29

WEB SITES

To learn more about the Pachycephalosaurus, visit ABDO Publishing Company on the World Wide Web. Web sites about the Pachycephalosaurus are featured on our "Book Links" page. These links are routinely monitored and updated to provide the most current information available.

www.abdopublishing.com

IMPORTANT WORDS

carnivore a meat-eater.

continent one of the earth's seven main land areas.

Cretaceous period a period of time that happened 144–65 million years ago.

fossil remains of very old animals and plants commonly found in the ground. A fossil can be a bone, a footprint, or any trace of life.

herbivore a plant-eater.

paleontologist someone who studies very old life, such as dinosaurs, mostly by studying fossils.

partial part of something.

predator an animal that hunts and eats other animals.

skull the bony part of the head that protects the brain.

theory an idea.

unusual different, or unlike other similar things.

31

INDEX